IT ISN'T EVERY DAY

IT ISN'T EVERY DAY

selected poetry by

David Mason Heminway

clamp down press
1999

The author gratefully acknowledges the following publications
in which some of the poems in this book were previously published:
Babel, First Class, Persephone, Shearsman, Le Balze
and the two volumes:
a bird in the bush & *Where the Bone is Green*

The editor wishes to thank the following people for their
help and advice with this book:
*Laura Savard-Bodwell, John Mitchell, Mark Matteau
& Scott Mullenberg*

Edited & Typeset by
Joshua Bodwell

Cover & Vingette Art by
Kevin Levasseur

Cover printing by
The Dunstan Press

Author Photo by
Tom Lipton

IT ISN'T EVERY DAY

ISBN 0-9672666-0-2 hardcover
ISBN 0-9672666-1-0 softcover

Library of Congress Catalog Card Number
99-070630

CLAMP DOWN PRESS
Post Office Box 7270
Cape Porpoise, Maine
04014-7270 USA

My thanks to Paul Cardaci, Josephine Jacobsen, Tom Lowenstein, Tamara Ralis, John Pfordresher, the patience of my editor, Joshua Bodwell and, of course, and forever, my wife-friend, Betsy.

IT ISN'T EVERY DAY: AN INTRODUCTION

I am, of course, honored to have been asked to write this intro-
duction, for "it isn't every day" that fate conspires to bring to-
gether two old friends and colleagues after a thirty year hiatus to
celebrate their enduring friendship through poetry.

I first met David Mason Heminway in 1965 when he arrived from
Italy to teach at the University of Maryland's Munich campus. His
second volume of poems *GUITAR IN TISSUE PAPER* had just ap-
peared, and among my fondest memories of our two years teaching
together was hearing David read, especially his counterpoint poems
which he read with his wife Betsy. But by 1993 when I journeyed
to Florence (via Munich) to teach at Georgetown University's Villa
le Balze, I had completely lost touch with David. It was then that
fate intervened.

On a connecting flight between Brussels and Munich I was sepa-
rated from my wife because I offered to help two older women
with their luggage, and the only available seat was beside a woman
who, I later learned, taught at the German University in Munich.
On the off chance that they might have met, I asked if she had
known a poet there named David Heminway. Surprised to hear his
name again, she told me that they had worked together on a book,
but that he had left Munich a few years before. She did, however,
still have his address and phone number it Italy. Soon after our
arrival, I called David who invited my wife and me to spend the
weekend with him and Betsy in their restored farm house in Bag-
gio. I was overjoyed, since I could ask him to read to my students,
but was saddened to learn that David, now retired, had all but
stopped writing poetry. Yet I decided to ask him anyway, hoping
that neither the resonant voice nor the lyric muse had departed
forever. After some initial hesitation, David, at Betsy's urging,
agreed. And thus was our friendship renewed, a friendship that has
brought delight to me, my students, and other Georgetown faculty
who have followed me to Italy.

The present volume is partly the result of the many readings
David has since given at the Villa, for each time he reads, he brings

new poems to share with his many young and enthusiastic listeners. For readers who know David's earlier poetry, some of the poems in
IT ISN'T EVERY DAY will seem familiar. The pure sensual delight, the fondness for word play, and the subtle use of internal rhyme in poems like WHAT IS DONE, FIVE FIGS IN A BLUE BOWL, and THE EASIEST VALENTINE will remind them of David's earlier love lyrics; and SILVERENA: SELF PORTRAITS, with it's double-voice lines, will recall the sound as well as the sense of his poems in counter point. But there is much more that is new and original in these recent poems, especially in those that explore the themes of aging and death.

To complement these new themes, David has found new forms to either shorten his poetic lines to create dramatic tension or lengthen them to open metaphysical spaces. His series of Italian poems on his neighbors in Baggio — poems like ONE TO TANGO, LODOVICO DIED, and MARIA — are highly dramatic pieces held together by his carefully constructed narrative. In my favorite, THE MEO, the narrator recounts Loris' journey up the mountain with Zia Rosa to pay his final respects to the poet's own son, Benjamin, who was the charcoal-maker Loris' last "meo" or apprentice. Shortening the lines to make the dramatic moment more vivid, the speaker tells us: "He came up the hill to the house/ and said: Where is he? Dov'è?/ We led him to the living/ room where the ashes were/ in a small covered box/ in the center of the sofa./ He entered/ and inside the door/ he thudded his knees/ to the brick floor – immobile/ rooted to stay/ while the woman stood, a/ night shadow in the door. And/ he said aloud Addio/ to his last Meo, bowing his head." Then in the next line the tension is eased by a careful juxtaposition: "Next December he too died/ the man Loris..." which moves the poem toward resolution: "Both/ now in the cemetery/ in the Holy Field/ some call it here – maybe going/ Holy Mountains: the boy's small voice echoing/ the words to drive the mule up/ the path into the woods: Avanti!" The poem ends with the speaker wondering if "Maybe even" the two, Loris and the boy, are not still sharing their food as they listen to "the charcoal pieces still pinging/ like clear crystal glass."

In another elegy, STARS AND SEA, David neither lessens nor sentimentalizes the grief which accompanies the death of a young man, but again sees it as a transformation of spirit toward another stage of being, as a "...rippling silent soaring out of sight." The themes of aging, death, and transformation are also celebrated in two metaphysical poems, THE SOLSTICE OF THE HOLY WHEEL IN DECEMBER and PROUST, ME AND THE SCHNEELOCH. Of the knowledge we gain from observing the turning of the "holy wheel," David writes: "So silence becomes/ more essential as knowing, than does the use/ of language to equate us to the moment and/ each other. The invisible music of the flute/ floating from the seated boy." Here the simple but powerful image evoking "invisible" music complements the previous complex statement on the power of "silence" as "language" and, like the juxtaposition of Loris' death to that of the "Meo" in the Benjamin elegy, helps to transform the poem into high art.

Of these recent poems, which in WHEN ON A SNOWING NIGHT David compares to gourds "hook[ed] in the ceiling of/ my mind to stay there swaying," he writes: "I particularize each moment/ in the snowing night/ before the first streaks of day/ can mar their pristine privacy/ from which they become for me form." As I read these lines and those that follow, I am powerfully moved not only by their easy flow and the originality of David's metaphors, but also by the thought that, were it not for that mysterious woman in black whom I sat beside on the flight to Florence in 1993 and who "just happened" to have David's address and phone number in Italy, these marvelous, sometimes stunning poems might not have been written, or as David says in the concluding line of WHEN ON A SNOWING NIGHT –"set down here out into the light."

In "Sailing to Byzantium" Yeats writes: "An aged man is but a paltry thing,/ A tattered coat upon a stick, unless/ Soul clap its hands and sing, and louder sing/ For every tatter in its mortal dress..." At age seventy-two my friend David Heminway continues to "sing and louder sing" his songs of love, loss, joy, and transformation in what is, I think, the most original and profoundly moving of his four volumes of poetry. Hopefully, we will not have to wait another three decades or for a chance encounter to convince him to continue turning life into words that become for the reader both song and art.

Paul Cardaci
Georgetown University

I

THE DEER AND THE CAMELLIA

Burgeoning pink rosettes which since
Christmas budded, the camellia opened
the window into spring. Every dawn
I spoke to it and it spoke back. I
loved it; and it kept blooming back
— But the seduction for me
 was the same for a sleek fawn doe
who came softly through dark mist
down the mountain to steal into
the yard below, pretending it had
no delight at all in that pink beauty
that gleaming dark shape, only merely
wanted to near, to nuzzle, nibble a
tiny bit what the calling night after
day had begged for in its unscented flowers
and shining leaves. So one dawn I woke to
the tree still up. still loving me, yet now half
naked, bare twigs of winter, shivering —
O I know. I know I know: the deer took
tenderly , standing in the dark, just
carried away the vital being that had called it
waiting there aloof in love wanting to be
consumed — even ravaged slowly under
burning stars — while I slept on, dreaming
that I waked to see it trembling still.

But am I poorer or richer to say: this beauty
was by beauty found in the longing night
to take the splendor of the day away — Who
can say?. . .Who can say. Who can say.

to honor the poet Keats

1

WHAT IS DONE

What can I do to you to prove
    that I do love you beyond
        the body proper. Of course
I love your nipples pink and pure
    your pubic hair, and even in
        public I don't deny your
eyelash which quivers shooting me
    with a light glance. But
    going or coming I love much
    more the way we inter
    twine our natural legs in
    a vineyard of desire to prepare
    our minds for the demise
    of body, the evanescence of
    brain, and the merger of our
    selves formless to be free.
To this will all the proof
    fall foolish as a word and
        heir to all that is permanent
beyond the grave thoughts
    and insipid lips we share now.

ONE TO TANGO

Attilio never married, but he loved
to dance the tango. And he loved to repair
shoes. One with the other, moving strongly,
smoothly, his face brown as the leather, his
hands square, his feet sliding and his eyes
watching the way he'd move his hands to
cut the piece to size, or the way his
feet would move, guiding him through the
other dancers, swaying dipping, straight,
a hand against the small of her back, there,
a pressure — now a turn, now at the heel, here,
and then away towards the toe. Attilio — He
made both as he knew that one became the other
(the shoe became the dance became the shoe)
and he moved in shy delight as the music played
or as at his small open window he sat, the rose
climbing there to open its petals under which he
watched them move — the mules, the men, the
women with the baskets, the children pell mell
down the stony path: he watched, he passed
the time of day, he closed the shutter and
went in to Zia Rosa: *il tocco*. But so he
left there the empty shoe, the dance floor
empty too where he'd tangoed to hold still the
turn the slipping of the sole transparent in the
rhythm that drew him on — turning, weaving, cutting
past the others and then with that direct stamp
of one foot and the other, the hammer of the
making of the moment to put together the sense
out of his blue eyes watching as he, going through
the way they all passed by, heard only the song.

FIVE FIGS IN A BLUE BOWL

I love to eat plump green figs,
split them tenderly open to suck
the pulpy red flesh — its feminine
inside, sensitive to the eating, that
groans like a laden tree snapping
limbs in a high wind. The blue
bowl is that exterior sea of sky
that beauty surrounding her fruit:
the way she walks and talks
and thinks and bathes her
philosophy in the morning
light, the way she feeds a child
curling into her breast. But it is
the reality of eating her most
moist red inner self that makes
me know in me how I am her in
me while only also being
the child beyond, fathering the
way I feel she encompasses
all one single moment, sweet
in my mouth, as I speak to that self
where she is ripe in the knowing.

STARS AND SEA

Perhaps it was the first time, that
impression, when I saw him in the evening
in the gloom of a half-dark room sitting
in summer-white shorts towards me to talk
or the music he liked, a cassette he played
me of the singing philosopher, or my hearing
about him like some shadow figure when he
was away; but no doubt, to me he had
an affinity with blue — deep dark black
blue — the kind at the bottom of the sea,
the kind in the farthest reaches of sky
beyond the sun into endless dark, lit only
silently forever with sprays of star points.
You could get it in the way his eyes
of a much lighter shade blue set on you —
in the way he grew quiet fading into the
music, becoming one with the waves of sound:
the ideas themselves a reality in his body.
This led him early to consider stars and, yes,
to watch the way the vast sea came and went in
eddying currents. It threw its life net
around him to study and learn in those
recesses where time appears eternal, and
space is expanded into galaxies upon
galaxies, and where every drop of water's
a breath of infinity. And so is this how
his life did not end, but only the body inert
in the net — as his own idea of blue, deep
dark blue, expanded outwards above the surface
and on — rippling silent soaring out of sight.

for Paolo in his death

5

THE SOLSTICE OF THE HOLY WHEEL IN DECEMBER

It is dark where the light wheel goes
down into the depths of what we cannot
remember but know existence is. You and I
we always touch in such places, and you
see the spokes of the wheel before you
speak whereas I'll often bare myself, I
being nude by saying, and find that the
turning of the spokes has pulled the wheel
past while I was talking. So silence becomes
more essential as knowing, than does the use
of language, to equate us to the moment and
each other. The invisible music of the flute
floating from the seated boy. I shall
wait then to speak until the spokes
become at last visible, light rays of sharp
shining joy; and then embedded with you, I
will sing the way the body now flows down
through the passage of the night to no
longer be dismayed about the ways we are
and are not because finally the fading or
forking flies into motes of seeing, more
remote than even we can imagine now when
drawn to the hub or released to the very
rim: we are only I and only you in only us.
It is the secret freedom, always ours in each
separate one, of course, like drops of water,
grains of earth, atoms of air — all elements
stand still in us as we move away from or
towards the grinding divine in all its
glory along the path of flesh and bones
where we live now as only here in form
to reflect upon the reality of this is.

19 ROSES

red, on 13 May, magic
without thinking guile —
or guileless superstition
past anticipation: 19
bold roses: old 12 plus
new 7. Perfect 10 and
man 9. A cabala — 19
for 19 months, known —
each a drop of blood
in her deep dreamed
voice there in a vase
as pale as lips, he as
silent as her washed hair
they there
they're here, even
their secret, given stems
into water out of earth
to live unfolding petal
by petal, a gradual day
time, night time, month
time into yearning year
time of their undying.
And the old man friend
stood rooted still,
jaw slack at the sight
of the way these 19 red
moments translated
there into here precisely —
in unthinking blood time
in 19 scarlet globules,
in 19 beats of the heart, at
the corner
in the hall entering
their house.

for Tamara and Fabrizio

STRANGE HOW THEY ARE:

she, the myriad depth of a starry night, and
he the imp playing inside a sunbeam — strange
their paths should meet, join, intertwine
at this point in time...like those angels
in the eye of a needle, laughing at us
standing around squinting, gawking in
our perspective of mind and matter. While,
strange, they, enwrapped in light rapture —
that kind of freely independent love of
their own natures in each other's ether —
shimmer in their bodies as air currents do,
and when they return, she with a mote from a
sunbeam in her eye and he with a halo of
stars, strange again, we think of them as
lovers desirous of constancy always to be to-
gether as we see them now in their being.

for Andrew and Cheryl
on their day of 5 November 1995

8

I DO NOT WANT TO INDULGE

the edge of my joy to glint
in the dark of your fear but
minding how we are bound freely
to tell the truth of our being,
I'll go on into the way we
even know the back of each other's
heart, vain in the art of
blood; sure, you deserve more
than this, but less too, because
however much we hug, we let
the flesh and bones alone to
wander into winter forests or
lie on summer lawns; as sure as
the silence we live in we do
not need to speak to tell our
ways of tip to tip turning
inside the quiet shining air.

REVELATION

wingèd one with floating hair
how eyeing you are to land
while air relates your love

>   protruding knees
>   precisely on the currents
>   of a promise reiterated;
>   but the surrogate of
>   twice told rhythms
>   throbs while fire unfolds

how the air enflamed in
boxes of bodies dissolves to
present angles of fish
nibbling at sweet smelling weeds
waiting

Where
the spread of the shadow
wings beats the eye without
reflection — the unfurled gaze
the preparation, the burst — all
stars in the dark with no fall.

IT ISN'T EVERY DAY

we get together
to get together
a poet & an artist
like today for
sure for instance
for them for ever
the muses are
dancing in delight
because as I say
it isn't every day
sun & moon shine
together, in splendor
the sea meets the
desert, horizons melt
& all into all
for one
slender
infinite
day.

for Joshua and Laura
on their day, 29 August 1998

NIGHT STREAKER NUDE

running near enough to flash
us seeing it savagely bright —
a seductive ball and tail of
light — a portend of all that
appears and challenges —
to baffle us in our ignorant
bodies, where our bliss is
to be inside the way we
see so that seeing is not
necessarily believing but
an arc of revelation
to make us gasp at what
we know and do not know
forever being here astride
this consciousness —
in part, time as it is
and in part, as all is, in
this comet gyre — so we turn
with our eyes to take it with
us inside our stone house,
closing the door on the starry
sky still unblinking yet weary
of the amazed upturned faces
when it is only doing what
it is — as, after all, are we.

for Haley Bopp 14 April 1997

DIAGNOSIS

poetry is a disease; it is a virulent
genetic-deep disease. It causes sickness
in all the tiny corpuscles of consciousness
and begins to spread through organs, vital:
the heart, the liver; then stomach, genitals.
There's only just so much that one can
stand without lying down to die. The
throes of a poem may strangulate, may
bleed dry, may suffocate — may disintegrate
all the intelligence of life which we've
so carefully kept. Keeping to our health
regime, pumping and dieting and sexing, and
O God working at the job of being just right,
just the image of our imagined self. And
then, along comes this poem. An ordinary kind
(who the hell let that in?) seeming almost
barely a greeting card at the corner store and we
you, I, they, all of us take the disease, catch
it as if it were indeed quite ordinary, that is:
all of us who can. But some of us O God help us
are strong, colossi, magnificent specimens, ones
so great that in our hairy healthy happiness
we can escape death, the change, the way
our mind is antisepticked, and we smile to
think that the poet thought this time the
disease would catch. We lay aside the poem. And
casually rise, undress carefully, reaching
to turn on the taps of the shower — the hot, acid
shower of our own truth; under this torrent we
scrub ourselves raw; and steaming the mirror,
we sing the old songs which we know we knew and
which do a lyric rebound from the shining tiles.
Afterwards we dry, all the parts — visible, invisible
public and intimate. So. So. So. Twisting, turning
patting the flesh, stroking the bones, caressing our

carcass and then, dry, we may pick up the open book
again. Same page. Same title. And with tingling skin
we may once more begin to read. Only this time we die.
Because without dying we cannot be reborn, and without
being reborn we cannot learn, and without learning we
cannot live. And so we die, over and over, before, after,
late, early, we leap to take in the disease of poetry.

INTERNETWORKING

If I were sure
of anything
so uncertain
as love,
I'd let you
know for sure
by Fax or e
(for erotic) so's
not to hear
back your
laughter,
the click as you
dele me, terminally
down. Because
the more I program
the form of you
bare on line
in my dark room,
the more my blood
cursors the screen
with windows to see
you, color dots
undulating you,
zooming to enter
you, permanently
saved on my hard —
The impenetrable code
of love comes to
give my love
a laptop world of
surety: its rounded
life is 3 D you
loving me
in a laughter
I've never
heard.

JERUSALEM REVISITED 1095-1995

MILLENNIUM: IN MATTERS

of being it seems to matter not
to be or not, but to bite
the bullet where the metal of
dentine white's destroyed down
to the pulp of pain, or to fight
the bull where the red sees itself
suddenly rage the wind and charges
from all ages in the arena of
eternity so as to pander time on
its back bleeding from mouth
to nostril, breathing in snorts,
leaving a trail of blood
seeding the sand with all sorts
of designs and spores of late
hate making half a dozen rough
arcs as we take our bows strung —
the arrows to pierce nicely such
fortunate knaves whose knives
now sheathed have cut into the
heart of that bullet which begins
to turn, spin, revolve, revolt
against the barrel and leaving it,
after air, dissolves itself in
matter, being like Jason's sown
teeth, armed to the glory of a
gory God sitting in shining clouds
of useless memory tomorrow because
yesterday, after all, the Mass
celebrated the massacre while
on flesh dead foreign bodies
inside silent walls, flies kept
buzzing in one black steady hum.

II

FOR MY GREAT NEPHEW JOSH

How unfair you are in
your fair self to bite your
teeth time and again into
the sandwich on the beach
squinting at the glinting
sea, pretending not to
notice that I love you
even when I get up hardy
and hardly a moment
later walk not race into icy
waves partly because I
too was you 50 yrs
ago if such exists now
unfairly fair and went
down to write my name
like yours in the sand
of the same windy shore.

WITHOUT END

For you who live inside
of poetry without seeing
your being in it, come now
into the center of the dark wood
where leaders falter and all
the way of determination
the points of the compass
become dead center, and
the nausea of non-existence
conquers every flick of an
eyelash. It can be so
it can. I have seen it in your
eyes as you insisted you wanted
to die, to subside from the
hole in the sky through which
you'd been enveloped into the
pitch black galaxy: there,
constantly, it was for you
eternal and consuming, my
own voice into your silence
painful, awful to hear as
if aching to your inner ear;
and so I stopped talking to
bring you flowers instead
for your heart and went away
weeping.

LEAVING US

If only the wild thyme grows in the garden
without tulips daffodils or plum blooms,
the wall outside the cracked and eaten house
where the windows watch, looking far then
turning in to catch us moving in the rooms.
You are my love proud cat while the mouse
pokes in the cupboard eating as in tombs
the tarnished kings and the weathered grain.

If only the birds cried in the garden
and sang like another bird in the night
without the sun to sing to, the star then
rising with other stars over the hills
black burned by the setting, like tar when
it curves running in the late spring. Like
you, my love, awake in the dark hills
walking, or waking from the bed of light
to the light through shutters after rain.

If only the fish by the plums in the garden
were drawn by us, something then of us
would stay inside and outside as we are when
the fruit that bloomed hangs to be picked
or the cats go over the gate of the garden.
All of these, the sound and the growing, of us
and our ways and we of them, mimicked
and mirrored in green and black, loved us
as fish swam, fruit fell, silent cats licked
leaving us like light to come back again.

THE SHEPHERD DIDN'T WANT
TO BE BURIED NOW

used to lying on the ground in brown corduroy
cap, jacket, brown baggy pants, boots, his
green canvas umbrella slung to the side,
his dog dozing, lazily, ears pricked, as
rocks, trees, grasses and leaves moved
circling around him in camouflaged center
as did the sheep, as did now the few black
figures around the grave. He would have liked
it. His own humor as if he'd ordered the
gravedigger clowns, one tall, skinny, pony
tailed, an earring —his first time with a
spade — the other all worry, business as
usual, another box to get in the hole. They'd
dug it, were digging as we arrived following
the lofted coffin, now with just the family
and me, they roped the box and with audible
instructions began to lower. No, no. Foot
end first, hold up on the head. And glinting
in the late October sun of morning, the
shiny pine box tilted, lowered slowly,
stuck: Up. Pull up I said! Pr. . .He almost
called him Prick, but remembering respect,
stopped. His own foot end down, the head high
above earth, everyone looking on now with eyes
wide. The son beside me made a step forward
to help with brawn, but then returned to
hug me to him. He had tolled the bell that
buried my son. The son who dead, laid out,
bloomed blood, just as from his fall, dead, the
shepherd still bled from his nose, a fly buzzing
near, waved away. Once more struggling up, the
coffin was resurrected. The worrier frowned
hard at the box. Now, easy does it, slow. Slowly,
he commanded breathing, you, you. Slow I said!
Here, rest a while. Come my end. Take the feet,

I'll do the head. They spradled the coffin passing
in leaps along high ridges of earth. Grappling the
ropes once more, this time they sweated to manage
almost, but the feet were up now, and the head
down. How that man loved to stand on his
head! Whenever he saw me coming he pulled out
the red flag to lure my bull: Ah, Americano,
what beautiful things Russia's doing. Such
dirty things America. Ah Americano, how nice
it would be to have you living here if only
you were Russian! And I played bull to him even
when one day late in December I found him up
in my holly tree. Ah, good, good, said the lead
clown digger. Now it's going. And the coffin sank
slowly inching, balking, but going down. Just as
he had come down out of the tree with an Oh, I
didn't know you were here. Brown face grinning:
Just some holly for my daughter in law. If I'd
known you were here I would have asked. How
could I explain to him except right now, here, that
being absent made no difference to being present.

We went forward now picking up handfuls of dirt
to bury him as he lay inside the box below.

THE MEO (the charcoal-maker's apprentice)

When the boy died, the man
came up the hill not
as he had come up with
heavy steps, a sofa on his back
and then the refrigerator, not
as he had later
come up one windy night
with his radio blaring
or down black-faced
from his carbon igloo,
not even as he had come
with a carved cane of
chestnut for the living
boy, nor as he came by
with the mule calling
at dawn the boy but
now he came up
with his neighbor an old
sere woman all in black
with a folded cloth
draped from her head — Zia Rosa.
He came up the hill to the house
and said: Where is he? Dov'è?
We led him to the living
room where the ashes were
in a small covered box
in the center of the sofa.
He entered
and inside the door
he thudded his knees
to the brick floor — immobile
rooted to stay
while the woman stood, a
night shadow in the door. And
he said aloud Addio

to his last Meo, bowing his head.
Next December he too died
the man Loris, who could, said
the boy, "cut wood like butter". Both
now in the cemetery, the Holy Field
some call it here — maybe going
into Holy Mountains:
the boy's small voice echoing
the words to drive the mule up
the path into the woods: Avanti!
Madonna mia, avanti! Maybe even
sharing food and the boy
bringing water to the blackened
figure resting in his wooden shoes
tired and dry after the work
the charcoal pieces still pinging
like clear crystal glass.

LODOVICO DIED

Today down the hills and through your woods
comes the strong wind of the mountains — la
tramontana — sweeping clean the sky. Young,
you carried bulging weights of charcoal
sacked on your shoulders the length of the field
to win second prize in Sardegna. "It was easy,"
you grinned sweating: "At home I rode my Maria
on top of the sacks!" — and in the same Sardegna,
you left your fore-finger, matcheted into the basket
with the logs for the *carbonaia*. All the strength
you had came out through your frame. I have
a movie I took later: you shouldering the
logs up here, making the circle, piling wood up
into the igloo. That was after the cement factory.
Husky work to carry those sacks through the powder
fog that settled into your lungs. Those years and
beyond, rasping, breathing in a fistful of air
for that brawny body of yours. You worked your
strength as always, smiling at us, moving slowly up
and down the mule path, doggedly giving us yourself
to stay and stay day after day in front of the TV,
pouring oxygen from tubes into your lungs to live —
without ever taking your eyes off the way
the sun slanted, the way the tree would fall,
the way the wind was blowing day and night
down the hills and through your woods.

MARIA

With your pretty French lilt, foreign, nervous
and saucy eyed, you flaunted a look to the village,
that made them tease you. "She isn't one of us,"
they said. "Arrogant girl!" Your skirt swung,
particularly modest, peculiar enough to catch
the eyes of the young blades who had tramped up
and down the hill path, mules loaded with wood
undulating the rocky way. And now they hung
at the fountain squirting each other, hosing arcs
of cold delight to laugh, shining teeth in the sun.
You waited with the other women old and young,
copper water ewers vinegared to glint in their
hammered hollows. You hummed a melody of Alsace,
and it was this ditty that caught Lodovico's ear.
He'd seen you high in a cherry tree reaching to pluck
the fruit; and in the shade of your doorstep
embroidering a snow white pillowcase with
a rapid needle. But now he knew. The next time,
in October, when some from the town had gone
up to your mother's woods to heave down bags
of chestnuts to the *seccatoio*, Lodovico piled three
on his shoulders to turn as he knelt, loaded already,
to you. "Want a ride?" he said. "Too much," you
said with that shy smile, more eyes than lips. But
Giacomo, his friend, came over: "Here, I'll lend you
a hand." He swung you in the air onto the top. And
before your mother or anyone else could say Stop,
Lovovico was up on his feet starting down the path
to the roofs of the town below. He lumbered, slowly,
a big bear of a man, and humble, you held
his hair, laughing all the way down to the shed.

ONE UP; ONE DOWN

Ten struck into the May morning,
sun and birds scintillating air, she
stepping from the Guidi's palazzo
in muted grey, her guards
resplendent in scarlet and blue,
then some twenty-six in entourage, and
her beagles. She was first, as always,
without fear; today decided for the
short-cut route up by Baggio knowing
this way bordered the bandit hamlet
some called Salvanaccio. "A fair day," she
said to the near but thought already
ahead to the monastery with Prior Bertoldo
on top of La Collina — the way it lay
wood-nestled, sheltered from the north,
the tramontana. Tomorrow on to the torrent
of Lucca arced by her bridge (everyone said
"impossible," and so they had too with
Henry) But it was done as that had been
done too as the Lord had let it be done —
the Devil agape. To La Badia now. The step
was placed next to her shiny black mule,
ears pricked up, alight with sunshine.
She took the hand proffered and even at
her age spryly ascended into side saddle.
His Holiness had once remarked: "Matilda,
if you bound upwards to Heaven as nimbly
as onto the back of your Genevieve,
you will get there long before I do."
And she'd answered directly: "If the Lord
so decides, I am ready." Now without
looking, without even a wave or nod, she
spurred, starting down the slight
slope towards the Gate of San Marco.

At the same hour he in his open-throated

shirt, sweating and grinning, sprang up
onto the burlap seat of his rusty orange
tractor, trailer loaded with logs, kicked
it to start even in gear. It bucked forward.
His wife on the ground with her mother and
his twig of a twelve year old son stood
watching as the tractor refusing gear, downed
the hill. Yelling his lungs out like the
day he was born, Renato shouted oaths
at himself, the tractor, the Virgin as he
found no brakes, roaring off, bounding into
the sunshine down the mountain. The tractor
jumped, wood and trailer banged, he strained.
The three stood helpless, amazed, gasping at
his jet descent, logs spewed in all directions
Renato ducked and held on going down.
Straight down.

        Matilda riding up, her
guards ahead, now, though she knew she did
not need them: already they had passed the
two mills of Mengarone grinding, and tight
shuttered windows of Salvanaccio. The way
up between close echoing walls had begun.
Genevieve's delicate hooves taking the path
with ease while the line of people behind
her swayed ziz-zagging, sometimes in the
spring air calling out to each other. But the
wimpled erect Countess of Canossa was quiet
glancing upwards to the tiny town coming
nearer, as Renato charged down.

        "I thought
him surely dead!" said his wife Carla later.
Brakes out, gears neutral, the square-set man,
crouched so's not to hit the tin roof, grasped
the wheel, urging this orange missile aside
before cornered into trees. Muscling his strength.

The Countess alighted at the Baggio fountain
to taste the gushing water. And went alone

into the wayside chapel — she never passed one by —
knelt, eyes closed, head up, to thank the
Lord for his kindness to her on her way,
and pray as always for those in distress.
She thought she heard indistinct noises far up
the mountain. She crossed herself and rose, once
more mounting to take her way up the mule path;
as Carla crossed herself seeing her husband crash
down the path: wheel still gripped, wrestling
the tractor, hurtling down the bumpy stones,
one moment working to pound the gear shift to low,
the next as if to leap free. But he stayed. His
head hitting now, body jolted and bruised, he
stayed. At last a walloping blow of his fist
jammed the gear down. It held. The tractor growled
grinding in protest, lurched, swerved from the dark
trunks, upped a bank, lost a wheel, flipped.
Stopped dead. His family crying out already
on the run. But dazed, bashed, Renato began
to crawl free. Alive! Alive! they wept. Crowding
to him to hold him safe. While still undulating
in the midday sun, Matilda clip clopped, languidly
swaying, slowly ever higher up the path to find her rest
for that night in the solemn forest of firs at the top.

La Badia is no more, the tractor neither; but the two —
one from Canossa, the other Baggio — remain (one alive;
one as legend) as do the stones of the mountain mulattiera.

AFTERNOON AT THE FALLS

It is dark afternoon when we arrive: Jesùs,
Carmen, Mattias, Colette, Nathalie the dancer,
and I, David, as different as our names
implying out roots to each other more than
speaking our languages of which no one speaks all —

But our laughter is common and our sweat, climbing
the mountains through the ginestra and the blackberry
bushes in the chestnut woods. The heat of the summer in
submerged air; but then comes the mountain Burè,
a stream falling in gushes and pools through uncleared,
empty woods. All others now in the city or at the sea.

Our joke at the first fork, the dried-up bed, takes: Damn
I say, they've copped the water at the top! Five dif-
ferent disbeliefs but all believing. The other path to
return, I say. We go on over the hillock and the falls
hurtle towards us. Hearing it we hurry tearing
off our clothes. I go in nude, I say. I clamber
up the dark rocks, green and red stains on their black.

No sun but the water white as moonlight pours down
itself. I go under. And another, and another, and then
two, and finally the last. They clamber up, their ochre
bodies passing and interweaving to the top, and return.
Some sit. We call in waterfall talk, we glisten
with clarity, we shout our wordless cries —
one after the other, united by the electric drops.

In the evanescent not having to explain. Without
philosophy inside the spray of time, stinging hearts
we love each other hopelessly: Jesùs slides on his ass,
Nathalie curves up the bank, Carmen hugs her knees, I
watch them spradle, flex inside this womb without death.

We dry. We come slowly, silently down the mountain path.

SILVERENA — SELF PORTRAITS

The silver self speaks out
of time where the babble of
birds becomes a single wing in
flight for we are not here as
we claim watching the interloping
light and shadow but are every
where when what we know is
not only us but you and it
remains the dot of shining
silver on its way into the ether
dissolving us quite
definitely designed by
the silver eye of self.

    *   *   *
             *

Silver ripples Silver
       living
       above
  be   be
       beyond
the flesh   of photo
         not
       covering
               re-
 vealing
distinct   formless
       idea,
self emerging self
to show   to show more
more
than   they
they   can
     imagine.

They
flare   in   anger
shading their eyes flaring
dark   against   light
          against
          Truth
always   always
so much   such an
   after   after
          after
          image

                    *
*   *   *

   The silver ripples
   living above, beyond
   the flesh of photo,
   not covering
   revealing distinct
   formless idea of
   self emerging to
   show more than they
   can imagine, in anger
   shading their eyes
   against the light.
   Truth has always
   such an after image.

   *   *   *

At the moment of leaving, she said:
You haven't seen my silver photos, and
beginning to explain how others, her colleagues,
her friends were angry with the result: Not
a photograph at all. You've covered it up.
And in the living room under wooden beams
on the bare wall they were wavering like
silk like water like air as one walked across

towards them. To stand still was for them
a transgression, to move with light was
their action. And she went on to explain
the technique turning about and taking
us across the hall to the work table: All the
elements of photography are here after all,
she said. All the elements of being, I agreed.
We said: Goodbye. It was not long before we
would see each other again, taking away the
transparency with us on the road in the night.

for Verena Gagern

THE WAY OF LIGHT

Without a source it would be dark —
maybe little pin points would let us
know that ultimate illumination waits
to be born in each one of us — a larger sun
to burn shadow, to bend its light
lovingly around each blade of grass,
caress rose and thorn, give us one blinding
moment of sight wherein our years
might again begin at zero to think:
If there were no light we'd be
phantom moon figures in a dusty
landscape of silence looking towards
a blue world across unmeasureable space;
and then, after the light comes, to know —
the instant its ray touches us — all
shape is different. Instead of floating
in limitless dark-sleeping velvet, we
will form the way we are by the way
it is: it will redefine the edges of
our being and we'll no longer
yearn after distant blue planets,
but discover here a nearer galaxy in
our own outline — what we were
is who we are. . .Seeing this all
because of light, and in its prism
hearing at last the sound of silence.

THE SKELETON

As long as I can walk or
hold these vertebrae erect
one on top of the other
piled precariously, a child's
building blocks wished
together, I can I hope hold
the idea of how that which is
inside me, even lying on
its back, can lope casually
into the dreadful dream, the
ebony ivory, the spacious all,
carrying its being along
with me in my perambulations
of this planet — a minor one
amongst many, but not yet
dead — for earth is still,
while whirling, a toddler's way
of having a place to stand.

III

THE SATYR ON THE TERRACE

prancing in the June sun behind
the knowing salamander eyes of
the old poet, has a fig leaf — I smile
but don't talk about the absence against
the big pricked find, erect in a river bed
of Siphnos, such a satyr of innocent joy
like the adolescent boys who today play
chess, backgammon, cards, still — inside
old Pharnos' sweet Cafe on the corner
under the grape trellis. It does not matter
that this satyr's mellowed in good taste so
as just to let her sit alone without being
prodded in her autumn dryness or scraping
her to feel more than how it used to be
now written on the walls of her memory
when he and she wandered amongst
the Karyatids, Greek wind blowing
their garments flat against their bodies,
while the Aegean sea pounded shores
ceaselessly — breathing all night long.

APHRODITE RED

titted
figure of love
out of the waves
armless
pursued by
a bug-eyed
smooch fish
out onto the
green steps
of the front
stoop

for Laura Savard

SAYING GOODBYE AT THE MILANO STATION

could not
include all
the hello's
we'd come
across,
shining stones
along the
path as
we lounged
talking
encapsuled
in
a foreign
city,
intimate in
ourselves
like being
there on
sofas,
sunk deep
into the
night,
knowing
we didn't
even have
to talk to
tell
the poetry
of
each other
and hear
it.

for Joshua

WHEN ON A SNOWING NIGHT

(It's actually dark dawn)
I have these poems one
after the other — these opening
lines   (Bold. Inane. Obsessive.)
hook into the ceiling of
my mind to stay there, swaying
from the beam (Ripe. Plucked.)
just harvested but not wanting
to shrivel dry hung up on those hooks —
I find I watch them fascinated
in their sway, turning one side,
the other, then returning back
beckoning to be inspected:
(eyed — thumbed — stroked)
until at last I toss aside
the night covers, groping
to collect myself (pen, paper, glasses)
moving by feel out into the
living space (leaving bed —
leaving wife and dreams behind).
I begin to take each gourd down
carefully from its hook: word upon
word into line upon line
holding them up now to examine
exactly (Shape. Size. Color.)
And precisely cut them open
scooping seeds and pulp
(in my scrutiny out of sleep)
I particularize each moment
in the snowing night
before the first streaks of day
can mar their pristine privacy
from which they become for me form:

(still up there in the dark and
swaying a little on their hooks)
but now in my hand and from it
(waiting murmuring insistent)
set down here out into the light.

FIGURES IN A ROOM

figures in a room, spare
contained like white fountains
light rising in miniature
to show how inside of glass
we are reflected outside
in large splendor where
these delicate bodies
are considered absurd
somewhat like water
as evanescent as quiescent
as towering as a tiny
second in a bubble
from a shining fish mouth,
or a white moth with iridescent
wings leaving light dust.

for Tamara Ralis

We are destined then
to be linked
only
in oils and ink
Meeting in the silverplated tick
of a wrist watch or
on the greyness of a sloping bench,
we are just two
excited hashes of freckles; we are
just two stems of unusually
willowy
niceties.
But, then, this is our way
with a pen
with a brush,
an eye and an ear,
(we do not need a mouth)
this is our way
to embrace all there is of
necessities, time
ourselves and
each
other.

for March Avery Cavanaugh

SONNET SUNSET

Naked winter limbs, lined with snow,
Remind me of the time when you were stripped
And stood out straight cold white once tip to toe
With me knee deep to plunge blue-lipped
Into that mountain stream in all the russet
Gold of autumn, while the sky of evening
Reflected in green water splashed us set
In nature when our eyes were still believing.
But we never talked of it, nor recalled
What you could tell to others and they
To me about the old and young who sold
Their right, refusing there one night one day.
Blameless is the arrow as the bow;
To each of us the sky in winter glow.

PROUST, ME AND THE SCHNEELOCH

In this snowy hole in the Alps where
I've been going for years, the lake is
living black, and sometimes the peaks
light up as if from inside, then fade
again to blue-white while I stand
often enough still — still as a black crow
on a snow-white branch, and spin out
my breath and words, visible frosty fog
into the quiet air — and on and on as long
as this breath will last (usually at
least one side of a page), not so much
with a thought as with the exhalation
of the moment through me into time
remembering not just the past
(no more did he though he called it that)
in millions of subtle constellations
of moments flying across the narrow
arc of sky, but the exhalation of all
that is outside coming into and
returning out of. This demands
silence — (as he knew and insisted)
— darkness too until it may be flashed
scintillating on one snowy peak, and then
one more. I learned this at another time
and in another language — (whether from
him or not and that reading aloud, I am
not sure; he'd know). But here
by this black sea — which reflects into
itself all the rising up of white sides
and on the rim of which black leafless
trees climb upwards with white snow —
by this living sea, I say, I have heard you
speaking to me in all the rhythms
of the deep long breath of life,

my friend; I hug you to me high
in these rarified mountains standing
watching, waiting, in the snow
as the crows now take flight by
the edge of white where it meets,
touches, the being of black icy water.

TRANSLUCENT

the lake came down to me
in its mountain image,
yellow green in evening;
I stood astride
legs under water,
which touched the globes
of the world to spin out
and up the side of the bank
on up into the sky. How
could the inverse of
me be there too? I
made no waves, no
ripples, but lay upon
the image, lay into
my reflection, and did not
look behind. Two years
and twelve days later
I told this to her as
we sat wearing straw hats
at a red table under the
chestnut trees after lunch.
And how did you like, she
said, your beautiful soul?
I swung to face the face
immaculately smiling into
my blue cast eyes. You are,
I said, as it is; and I am
as it is. I've come away
only with my reflection
which here before you
is, as you can see, me.

AN OLD MAN POET

has come to live in our
house. Under the eaves he
wanders the day away in
his oldness; and
as poet, writes the night up
into dreams; but it is
the man of him that arcs —
rocks between the two
stars of his being. Whichever
I admire of the three
circled into one, I watch
in almost awkward stupor
seeing it through his
glass — the fine white
words pouring down with
a faint echo of the vast sea
down the narrow waist, on down
through the filter of his heart

THE EASIEST VALENTINE

If there ever were a Valentine that
would suit you, I'd buy it, buy
the heart, buy the flowers, buy
but I can't find you in a shape;
And I can't find me to you in words
because I mean to be loving you
not in constancy as I've always stopped
and ever explained but in change, a May
Pole in winter with all the red threads
tight, tied, broken, chained which
keep us single as we look direct
into each other's iris blooming there
mirrored in the mirror of their color
of violets, the pungent kind we've picked
the paper kind in the easiest Valentine
blue, yes, the color of infinity, of
Grecian seas, of death – the color of truth.

RUSSIAN POETS USED TO

read in arenas all night, with vodka breaks
& pit stops, until the dawn came in from Siberia
to take them unawares onto the shoulders
of the crowd: a some-kind-of-football hero
who has passed the ball a thousand times
over the heads to score goals; or maybe
a glittery rock star stomper to whom the
audience stampedes, lighting lighter flames
to heat the heart.
                              But we American poets?
Well, we sometimes break away to coffee-house
ourselves, of course, or pull the university
circuit, but often duly spread our words across
the soundless void of uncompromising white
space — as cold as that Siberia, as ruthless.
Only when we sleep do we read all night
(American counterpoets: one language for all)
all night to ears we have invented in which the
religion of listening extends beyond
the seat where you sit, into the far reaches
of the darkness and all the inflections like
waves on beaches flow into you, through and out —
and on into the farthest death you can imagine
where you can live one black night in the extremes
of sound as light before the weak dawn appears.

MANTIS AND BOY

In the early morning after
he'd hopped like a grasshopper
and fallen to bloody his head, he
saw a mantis on a spear of grass
in his grandfather's garden.
The mantis stood up to pray
with his green arms and the boy
coaxed it to his shoulder. He stared
intently pushing his face near
Look, he said with joy, Look at
the praying mantis. He has four legs and
then two skinny arms. He eats grasshoppers.
Seriously. But just the little bit
of meat, not the whole grasshopper. Other
insects like the rest. Like for instance
the dragonfly eats all the other parts.
And he set back down gently his arm
into the grass. He sat on his haunches
in the sun, his red hair copper flames,
to inspect and wait. Maybe he's not hungry.
He ate breakfast already. He looked up at
his bearded grandfather: You know what? My
head just doesn't hurt any more at all.

Living in the Pistioa mountains, Heminway and his wife
keep busy: making gardens, cutting wood for two stoves, having
guests, tickling the tummy of yellow-eyed Pardo. . . .
and holing up to write.

COLOPHON

The first edition of
IT ISN'T EVERY DAY
consists of 500 perfect-bound into
paper wrappers and hand-numbered;
26 hand-sewn into clothwrapped boards.
These 26 copies (lettered A thru Z) have been
signed & thumbprinted by the author and
contain a signed linocut print by the artist
Kevin Levausser.

The zygote of this book was born
one warm July evening in the publisher's
tiny office on Cape Porpoise harbor, when poet and
publisher sat up late into the night, talking.

The text has
been thoughtfully set in
11pt. Caslon, with titles in
12pt. Caslon Open Face.
The cover display is Goudy's
30pt. Hadriano Stone Cut.

168.